Nursing Ourselves

WHILE NURSING OTHERS THROUGH A PANDEMIC

Nursing Ourselves

While Nursing Others Through A Pandemic

Helen Bhagwandin

XULON PRESS

Xulon Press
2301 Lucien Way #415
Maitland, FL 32751
407.339.4217
www.xulonpress.com

Printed in the United States of America.

Paperback ISBN-13: 978-1-6628-1403-7
eBook ISBN-13: 978-1-6628-1404-4

Preface

I dedicate this booklet in honor of all my nursing colleagues and healthcare workers: For those who have gone on to be at rest and to all who are still on the front line, many of whom were students of mine, who are now in the fight for a pandemic-free environment. The purpose of this meditation booklet is to be a resource and support for our nurses on this unprecedented journey; one that can travel with them and be readily available in times of need. The intent is to remind them that they are on a special mission and never alone. Also, this booklet reminds them that there are times they must ask, seek, and knock and do whatever it takes to stay safe, yet vigilant, on the journey. Nurses are very much concerned about the care of the whole person, mind, body, and spirit when caring for their patients. However, too often nurses neglect to care for themselves in that same manner and, thereby, disregard their need for spiritual nourishment and refreshment. Therefore, the focus of this book is self-care for the caregiver, even while giving care to others.

The meditations are numbered and not dated so that whatever the need is for that day, which may be the same as the day before, it can be used again. With much consideration for nurses' time, the meditations are short and simple. Each meditation has a supportive Scripture verse and a prayer. The focus is on many of the needs that have been expressed to me by those on the frontline, whom I have reached out to, so that I may provide emotional support and encouragement.

At the beginning of the pandemic, I wanted so badly to be out there on the frontline with my colleagues. However, I was classified as being in the high-risk category. In expressing my feelings of helplessness to my friend Connie, a retired faculty member, she assured me that I was already out here in the many students I had prepared for a time as this. This was truly an eyeopener and a consolation for me since I taught the care of critically ill patients in the intensive care unit and the emergency room.

Table of Contents

Whom Shall I Send: Here am I, Lord, Send Me

Some of you heard the call many years ago, some not so long ago, but whenever it was, you responded to the call with "Here am I, send me"; and here you are in the call of your life. It is a call you had no idea would take you on such a journey. Yes, you responded to a calling and not a job. A call to service, one of compassion and caring, whereas a job is a service that is paid for; however, no pay can suffice the things you do for humanity. You do things for others who cannot do those things for themselves. You save lives while risking yours and risking the health of your families. No one can pay for the uncharted contribution and caring you give. Caring can never be measured or quantified, even though acts of caring are documented. However, real caring is grounded and rooted in the heart and soul of the caregiver.

And I heard the voice of the Lord saying, "Whom shall I send, and who will go for us?" then I said, "Here am I! Send me" **...Isaiah 6:8**

Dear God, Creator, and Healer of all instill in me a caring heart and may I be reminded that it is Your work I have been called to do... Amen.

#2

Who Am I?

I am a child of God and an inheritor of the Kingdom of Heaven. I am someone special, and I have been called to a special service. Today, I will do what I have been called to do. Today, I will care for every patient as if that patient were my mother or father or sister or brother or any beloved member of my family. That is what I have been called to do, and to do so to the best of my ability. I will respect the dignity of all people, for everyone is a child of God as I am. However, I seek God's guidance to do all that I need to do, knowing that there are times when I will do all that I can; times when I will have done my best, and yet I must draw back and let God do the rest.

This is my commandment that you love one another as I have loved you. **John 15:12**

Dear God and Father of all, grant me the gifts of patience, endurance, and a heart to love my neighbor as You love me.

#3

Self-Care

I am aware that to give the best care to others, I must first care for myself so that I can give the best of myself. Self-care is taking care of my whole being: body, mind, and spirit. This is the care that I intentionally plan for all patients in my care, which I will now give to myself. My body is the temple of the Holy Spirit; therefore, today, I will take good care of my body to be worthily receptive to the Holy Spirit. Today, I will promise to care for my body by eating properly to get the right nutrients to nourish and replenish the cells of my body. I will intentionally plan my day to get adequate rest with a good night's sleep. I will also make time in my daily schedule for physical exercise to support my mental and physical wellbeing, as I will await a new burst of energy and enthusiasm for my day.

Do you not know that your body is a temple of
the Holy Spirit within you, which you have from
God? You are not your own... **1 Corinthians 6:19**

Dear God, I thank You for a body so beautifully
and wonderfully made and I thank You for all
the blessings of this life. Make me ever grateful
and caring for my body, which You made in
Your image and for Your temple. ...Amen.

#4

Cultivating A Positive Mindset

Today, I will make quiet time to be at peace in response to the invitation to be still and know God. I will seek out a quiet place and purposefully create a peaceful environment, using whatever tools to aid in creating this moment in time to quiet my spirit, as I prepare myself to meditate on God's presence. A session of mindful, deep breathing will allow me to relax. I then release all concerns or lingering mistakes of the past. I will be gentle and forgiving of myself, as I affirm peaceful, loving thoughts of myself in the presence and care of my Creator. As I visualize and sense God's presence, I feel the love, joy, and peace that I need to carry me through the day and to be reflected in all that I do and say. I will stay mindful in maintaining this serenity throughout my day. I pledge that throughout this day, I will feed my mind with positive thoughts that will attract positive responses in all my relationships, and in all that I do, and from all whom I meet.

Finally, brethren, whatever is true, whatever is honorable, whatever is just, whatever is pure, whatever is lovely, whatever is gracious, if there is any excellence, if there is anything worthy of praise, think about these things... **Philippians 4:8**

Heavenly Father, I thank you for allowing me to come into Your presence. Thank you for forgiving me and freeing my mind of concerns of the past; and for infusing into my being Your spirit of love, peace, and joy to share with others, as Your light shines through me ...Amen.

#5

Nurturing Supportive Relationships

I n caring for myself, I embrace friends who are there with me to share this journey that only they can understand; friends who will hold my hand when I need that reassurance, as I, in turn, will hold their hands to give assurance of better times to come. Yes, we too need to have our hands held, as we so often hold the hands of patients who need comfort and assurance of healing, which may not be physical but a healing of the mind and spirit. As we become channels of God's love, peace, and healing, we are reminded that we too need God's blessings of love, peace, and healing so that we can better channel these gifts to God's children. Therefore, I open myself to God to be filled and recharged with these blessings to share with whomever, whenever, and wherever. I ask God to use me to be a blessing to my friends, as they continue to be a blessing to me. I am honored to be a part of God's circle of love and healing to family, friends, neighbors, and all who are in my care.

Two are better than one because they have a good reward for their toil. For if they fall, one will lift up his fellow; but woe to him who is alone when he falls and has not another to lift him up. **Ecclesiastes 4:9-10**

Dear God, I am thankful for all my friends. I come this new day with open hands and a willing heart, receptive to Your many blessings and ready to share your love with all You will place along my path this day. Amen.

6

A Call to Serve

Today, I commit myself to God to be ready for whatever is planned for me on this day. I am prepared for my mission. Dear Lord, if I must be the last one to hold a hand that is too weak to hold mine, then give me strength. If I have to say the last goodbye, because no family visitation is allowed, give me courage. If I have to offer the last prayers, because no chaplain is around, then give me wisdom. If I must close the eyes for the last time because all strength is gone, then give me peace in knowing that You work through these hands, as I am Your hands on this earth; for You, O Lord, have given me holy hands. May my role in this precious assignment be pleasing in your sight, as You welcome this soul into Your kingdom (Paradise).

Comfort, Comfort My people, says your God.
Isaiah 40:1

*Thank You, Lord, for opportunities to do
for others what they cannot do for themselves.
Thank you for strength, courage, wisdom, and
peace to face the challenges of this day...Amen.*

#7

Family

I have been blessed with a wonderful family to support and love me. My family is the most precious gift God has given to me. I want to be the best parent and spouse ever. I want to be there whenever my family needs me. However, many times I feel that I am not living up to what is expected of me, because there are times when I want to, but cannot, be there with my family. I trust God to care for my family and to guide and protect them while I am away from them. At the end of the day, when I return home from work, I am so elated to see my family, even when the mission of the day leaves me fatigued and sometimes drained. My family is the source of my strength and renewed energy. I give God thanks for this wonderful gift of family.

Have no anxiety about anything, but in everything by prayer and supplication with thanksgiving let your requests be known to God. **Philippians 4:6**

Thank you, God, for blessing me with a wonderful family. Make me always thankful to you for this gift and grateful to my family for their love, support, and joy that they bring to me from You. AMEN.

#8

A Blessed Profession

Over the years, I have come to realize that where I am is where I was meant to be. I think of all the directions I could have taken my life; other careers I could have chosen, and the other careers that I have been attracted to. In doing so, I recognize that I have been rerouted by a greater power than my own. I have been led to seek out and to choose a career for service to humanity: one of giving with compassion, caring, and ongoing commitment to give of my best. Caring, compassion, and commitment are gifts from God: I am honored to be blessed with such gifts that I can share with others. I am grateful to be in a career of service to others, knowing that Jesus Himself walked this journey serving others; and here I am, completing the work that Jesus started here on earth. This work is in the practice of healing, caring, and teaching. I am reminded daily that I have been called to do what I do and that I have been chosen and appointed to care for the children of God.

You did not choose Me, but I chose you that you should go and bear fruit and that your fruit should abide. **John 15: 16**

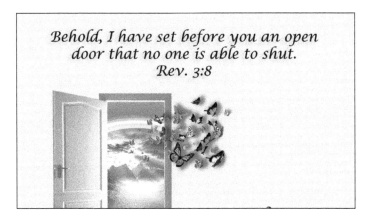

Behold, I have set before you an open door that no one is able to shut.
Rev. 3:8

Dear God, You have called me to a service of caring with compassion and commitment. I thank you that You continue to guide my actions and my humble service... Amen.

9

Finding Peace.

I know that no matter how busy and chaotic my day may get, I must make time for a mental, physical, and emotional refreshment. In times like this, I withdraw to a place of peace within myself; and as I come into the holy presence of God, I am intensely aware of how refreshing that can be. There are times when there might not be any such physical place, but I can step aside, close my eyes, and, in my mind, be emotionally and spiritually in that needed place. And in that place, I feel safe, knowing that I am in God's presence and this alone brings me peace. I freely let go of concerns, fears, and the burdens of ethical conflicts and decision-making. Oh! What a relief it is when burdens are lifted in this realm of peace and serenity. In returning to my previous state of awareness, everything that might have seemed chaotic before is now peaceful and serene. Peace resides within and resurfaces when fear, anxiety, and negative feelings are released. I continue to incorporate that peace in all my care.

For God is not a God of confusion but of peace...

1 Corinthians 14:33

Thank you, Lord, for allowing me to come into Your presence to be recharged and renewed so that I can find peace, even in chaos...Amen.

#10

Empowerment Through Prayer

I n the business of the day, I may get so overwhelmed with activities requiring fast decision-making. Some decisions may involve life and death situations, and I may become distracted from whispering a prayer. I am then reminded of the importance of relying on my Higher Power: for guidance in what I do, for wisdom to make those decisions, and for the courage to do what I need to do. In those quiet moments of prayer, there is the power to transform me from stress to calm, from confusion to clarity of thinking and decision-making, and from timidity to boldness. Yes! I emerge empowered to be all that I can be and to give the best of me in that place and time. I am so thankful that there is nothing that I must do alone on my strength, but I can do all things through the One Who strengthens me.

Be strong and of good courage; be not frightened neither be dismayed; for the Lord, your God is with you wherever you go. **Joshua 1:9**

Heavenly Father, I thank you for keeping Your promise that You will never leave me alone and that I need never be afraid, for You have given me a spirit of boldness...Amen.

#11

God as Protector

I f ever there was a time to be aware of the need for my safety and the need for protection, it is now. Today and each day, I give thanks for God's protection for my family, all my loved ones, and myself, as God takes us through the turbulence of this pandemic sea. I pray also for the protection of all patients and especially those entrusted to my care. I envision a hedge of protection surrounding us all, as only the almighty, omnipotent, omnipresent God can do. I trust God to take me through this day, knowing that wherever I am, I am not alone; for God's presence is always with me. This is so reassuring to know that I am never alone in this boat sailing the pandemic sea. Whenever there is the slightest concern for my safety, I reflect on a childhood chorus that **reminds me that I can sail through any storm with, Christ in my vessel.**

Be strong and of good courage, do not fear or be
in dread of them: for it is the LORD your God
who goes with you; he will not fail you or forsake.
Deuteronomy 31:6

*Keep watch, dear God, over all Your children
and keep us safe during these perilous
times... Amen.*

#12

God as My Provider

As I focus on the unconditional love and care of our God and Father for all His children, I pray that God will supply all our needs according to His riches in glory. In reflecting on the Lord's prayer and asking that He would give us our daily bread, I recall that many of our brothers and sisters, and even many of our colleagues, have had their daily bread taken away in the course of this pandemic. During this time, I am also reminded that I too can do my part by helping in my small way to contribute to those agencies and centers that provide food, clothing, and shelter for those in need. We are all blessed by our Provider to be a blessing to others in various, needed ways.

And my God will supply every need of yours
according to His riches in glory in Christ Jesus...
Philippians 4:19

Dear God and Father, thank you for supplying
all my needs; make me always aware of the
needs of my brothers and sisters, that I may act
accordingly through Your will…Amen.

#13

God My Strength

There are times when I may feel that I am not strong enough to continue in my role as a caregiver. I feel emotionally and physically drained. I feel like I have given all that I have and all that I can give. I may feel that nothing is left of me but a desire to coil up and go into retreat. I want to escape somewhere far away from everything around me. However, instead of a physical withdrawal, I enter my personal retreat space within myself, and there I am reminded of who and Whose I am. With this awakening, I affirm that I am a Nurturing, Unyielding, Resilient, Strong, Essential servant of God: Yes, this is who I am. My strength is renewed and I am energized, as I am daily reminded that my strength comes from my Maker and is renewed every morning. Here I am, Lord, strengthened, renewed, and ready for the mission of the day.

My strength comes from the Lord, the Maker of
Heaven and earth... **Psalm 121:1**

*Thank you, Lord, for each new day and for
recharging my body, stimulating my mind,
and giving me an enthusiastic spirit to face the
day... Amen.*

#14

Journaling

I may have a lot going on in my mind and in my life, which tends to clog my thinking at times. This may be during those moments when I have no one to share with; like during those wee hours of the morning and late nights. Therefore, I go to another source to clear my mind, and that is to my journaling. Here, I pen all my heart's desires, thoughts, concerns, and gratitude for the blessings of the day. For me, this is a form of praying and communicating with God. This journaling practice helps me to feel relieved, unburdened, and relaxed. Then I sit quietly in God's presence and listen, hoping to hear the still, small voice. I give thanks for the quiet time to be able to do this. I can do this anywhere if the need and the time to do so is convenient. Journaling can be a most expressive way of sharing some of our innermost secret fears and concerns. There may be some things that are hard to say or express but can be easily written. I give thanks for these various tools of communication and stress-releasers.

For God alone my soul waits in silence...
Psalm 62:1

Dear God, thank you for hearing my plea, whether I pray, write, sing, or sigh. Thank you for listening and teach me to listen in return. Amen.

#15

Finding Joy

J oy can be so hard to find in this tumultuous era we are going through at this time. However, I remind myself that to balance my life, I must intentionally seek out joy. Therefore, today, I look for joy in all that I do, even when the challenges of the day seek to ruin my joy. I think of all the joyous events that are happening: the new births of family babies; the graduates we had this year, within our families and friends; the Serenaders all over the world who have cheered us on; that patient on the ventilator you may have prayed so hard for, who did walk out; and what joy and validation for the work you do. Sometimes we have to think back to pre-COVID times when we participated in celebrations with friends, family, or colleagues. These are precious memories of joyous times; I hold on to these reminiscences of joyous times to carry me through this period in my life. I even sing some childhood choruses like **the one about having joy down in my heart to stay.** Yes, joy is there in our hearts; we just have to go deep sometimes to wake it up. What a joy it is when we can do so.

The Joy of the Lord is my strength ...

Nehemiah 8:10

Dear God, You are the joy of my life. Thank you for the love of family, friends, and neighbors all who bring Your love to accentuate my joy... Amen.

#16

Patience

Whether at home or at work, today I will intentionally strive to be patient with others and with myself. I find it is easier to be patient with others than with myself. I pray for patience with myself: with new equipment; with the length of required care for healing; and all those factors that prolong my predictive times for meeting certain goals. I remind myself to be patient when certain goals are not met, especially goals concerning the healing process, which delays connecting patients with families once more. However, I am reminded that times for healing are set by God, despite my predictions. With patience, I then open my mind and spirit to healing that is determined by God and in God's time. The length of time on a ventilator might seem excessive; time for elevated labs to reverse may seem extensive. However, I am reminded that healing is taking place, that all healing is not just physical, and does not always result in a cure. The final call is beyond my control and understanding, so I fully accept and do all that I know to do to patiently wait on God to bring about the best results.

Be patient in tribulation, be constant in prayer.
Romans 12:12

God, grant me the serenity to accept the things I cannot change, courage to change the things I can, and wisdom to know the difference. Amen.

#17

Enthusiasm

K nowing my purpose in this life, and knowing that I am called to my purpose, I welcome this day with enthusiasm. Despite whatever obstacles that may come my way, enthusiasm will carry me through this day. I am called to serve and to care; that is what I do and will continue to do. I seek my direction, guidance, and protection from my Creator and the Master of my life. Today, I entrust my family and loved ones to the best of care, as I go to deliver the best of care to someone else's loved ones. I am passionate about what I have been called to do and for the tools that I have been gifted with to accomplish my mission: wisdom, knowledge, understanding, and skills in healthcare. I give thanks for the divine guidance to implement the needed skills for each patient in my care.

Never flag in zeal, be aglow with the Spirit, serve the Lord. **Romans 12:11**

Thank you, Lord God, for a spirit of enthusiasm to do the work You have called me to do... Amen.

#18

Courage

C ourage is what I demonstrate each day when I wake up and leave my home and family to share my gifts with others. These may be persons I have not yet met, but I am willing to care for them, knowing that they are children of God, needing God's healing grace. I am prepared with the skills, the faith, and the courage to let God use me to be a vessel of this healing process. Courage is a gift and a blessing in this unprecedented time of this pandemic. Courage allows me to let go of concerns and doubt in what I do so that I can facilitate an environment of healing and assist patients to achieve optimal health. Courage is also noted in my willingness to face new challenges. These challenges consist of new illnesses, new diseases, new disease-causing organisms. New challenges also arise in managing care under new guidelines, policies, and procedures. I pray for courage to knock out the Goliath that roams this earth, as I pray for the right stone for my sling of skills to help each patient to win this battle of the pandemic.

For God did not give us a spirit of timidity but a spirit of power and love, and self-control. **2 Timothy 1:7**

Dear God, You know all things, see all things, and can do all things. Grant me the faith to trust You and the courage to do as You direct me to do, through Thy dear name...Amen.

#19

Prayers of Memory and Healing

Today, I give up a prayer for all my colleagues who did not survive this pandemic. These are colleagues who have been welcomed and ushered into the heavenly kingdom, where earthly angels make their final dwelling. May these dear, angelic souls rest in peace. I also pray for the return of health and wholeness for colleagues who are presently struggling to survive the battle of COVID-19; for those colleagues who survived, I give thanks for their healing. For those who have gone on, I am grateful for their lives and the gifts of the skills and talents that they possessed and shared with us. They have shared their gifts in various ways to make this world a healthier place. For those of us who are still in this battle, I pray for continued courage, strength, and protection; that we will be conquerors in the end, which I pray is soon, dear Lord, soon as to be determined by You, our Savior, Redeemer, and Healer.

We will always remember them, for they are part of us.

That they may rest from their labors and their works do follow them. **Revelation 14:13**

Thank you, Lord, for the various gifts and talents You have blessed us with, and in various ways. Amen.

#20

Leaning on Faith

M y faith has been a pillow of strength to lean on through all my life experiences. I am most grateful to be grounded in a faith that strengthens my resolve to serve others and to respect the dignity of all humankind. My faith is what I especially draw on in times of stress, anxiety, fear, or any type of chaos. Because of my faith, I remain hopeful during these unprecedented times, knowing that this time will pass as I look forward to new horizons. Many of the prayers and readings of my faith teachings are such sources of comfort during these moments. How reassuring it is to read such verses like "*I will never leave you or forsake you,*" and from my countless reflections and affirmations, as found in the 23rd Psalm, such as, "*The Lord is **my** Shepherd **I** shall not want.*" I feel so empowered, supported, and protected, as I recall these powerful teachings of my faith. Faith assures me that despite the chaos, all will be well.

Now faith is the assurance of things hoped for, the conviction of things not seen. **Hebrews 11:1**

Dear God, in You do I put my trust, as I lean on Your never-failing promises...Amen.

#21

Gratitude

I am most grateful for a new day with new opportunities to serve, to love, and to care. In gratitude, I hold up my family, friends, and colleagues who will love and support me through this day, as I also appreciate, love, and care for them. I am grateful for the chance to care for myself and to refresh my mind, body, and spirit to give my best self to the care of others. I am thankful for my place of employment, where I have the opportunity to do what I love to do, while I am also able to contribute to the financial support and welfare of my family. I am also in a place where I find opportunities: for growth; for learning, sharing, and collaborating with colleagues; for the improvement in care and service to all humanity. I am also grateful to be practicing my career calling in an institution whose mission and vision concurs with my beliefs and values. In gratitude for these many blessings, I rededicate myself to the service of all humanity.

O give thanks to the Lord, for He is good; for His steadfast love endures forever! ... **Psalm 107:1**

Thank you, Lord, for all Your blessings on me and also for a grateful heart to forever thank You, to praise You, and to serve You...Amen.

Solace in Turbulent Times

Create silence in a moment, to sit quietly and focus on breathing while trying to relax and soothe a turbulent spirit from all the emotional trauma of the day. A day of ethical conflicts, when difficult decisions had to be made regarding critical care requirements: bed shortage, staff shortage, equipment shortage, and shortage of personal protective gear. Amid all this is the constant noises of alarms from the ventilators and the various monitors. It is now time to settle in and prepare for a good night's rest. It is time to unwind and, therefore, release the suppressed whirlwind of emotions that dominated the hectic day. It is now time to discharge these emotions into the abyss of negative memories and to replace them with a comforting spirit of tranquility and calmness.

And He awoke and rebuked the wind and said to the sea, "Peace be still" And the wind ceased, and there was a great calm...... **Mark 4:39**

Dear God, hear my prayer and renew a right spirit within me... Amen.

#23

Available: On-Call

On-call duty has become more frequent during these extraordinary times of the pandemic, due to increased patient load, decreased staff, and unavailable patient beds in neighboring facilities. Therefore, it is time to call on one's inner strength to prepare physically, mentally, and emotionally: to be ready for whenever the time comes to respond to that crucial call. Now for whatever the task may be, it is one of service; a call to care for a child of God who is also loved by someone. Again, affirming the role of a Nurturing, Unyielding, Resilient, Strong, Essential servant of God. Yes, one who is, therefore, emboldened to follow this calling and to respond to the need to serve. It is further reassuring, knowing that God is in charge and cares for the caregiver as much as the one who needs care. Therefore, all concerns and needs are safely in the Lord's care and keeping, and are, therefore, well kept.

Truly I say to you as you did it to one of the least of these my brethren, you did it to me...

Matthew 25:40

Thank you, O Lord, for directing my path and calling me to serve Your people... Amen.

#24

Continued Learning

I commit to ongoing learning to keep current with new knowledge, to learn new skills, and to sharpen old ones. This enables me to perform at my optimal capabilities, to provide the best of care to my patients. Ongoing learning is a must in healthcare. This is not only for personal growth but also a requirement to maintain a valid license to practice. Being prepared and knowledgeable increases self-confidence and readiness to respond when called. Not all learning is formal teaching. Much of our learning is from day-to-day experiences, and also from other colleagues and sometimes patients. It is important to be open to learning, because the persons we least expect to learn from may have something to offer to our knowledge base. My learning is not always professional; many times I learn new information from my family, especially children who are readily available to teach something they learned. Learning can be fun, especially when young ones think that their aging parents are too old to learn about certain matters that are happening in their time. I give God thanks for precious learning moments.

The fear of the Lord is instruction in wisdom
Proverbs 15:33

Thank you, Lord, for opportunities to grow in knowledge, wisdom, and understanding to better care for Your children. Amen.

#25

Self-Healing

E ven though I am an agent in the healing process of others, I too need healing. I need God's healing grace to be a healthy vessel as a conduit for healing. Therefore, my daily plea is that God will bless me with a healthy body, mind, and spirit to be of total health and wholeness to serve. Our Lord yearns for us to be healthy and whole; I affirm this as I reflect on Jesus's many miracles of healing. Many of our healthcare personnel have been traumatized during this pandemic. Some have been traumatized mentally, some physically, and some emotionally, and some all three. Some of these colleagues have even moved on to use their skills in other areas. I send positive thoughts and prayers for them. I pray for God's healing on them, as God guides and directs them in the way they should go. I also pray that they may find healthy environments in which to practice safely while utilizing their knowledge and skills, as they return to full health and wholeness. I am daily reminded of the importance of staying healthy, not only for myself but for family, friends, and colleagues.

Heal me O Lord, and I shall be healed; save me,
and I shall be saved; for Thou art my praise ...
Jeremiah 17:14

*Thank you, Lord, for Your healing grace,
as You use me in Your healing plan for
others. Amen.*

#26

Living with Hope

My faith in God enables me to be hopeful. In being hopeful, I let go of any feeling of despondency and hold on to hope, which takes much perseverance and patience at times; like sitting and awaiting the results of a national election with great expectations. Hope infuses me with the resilience to keep on going and expect the good, the better, and the best from any situation. I am hopeful for my patients, my family, my country, and also for the world as we wrestle with this pandemic. I have learned that hope is always with us in the ever-present Supreme Being, the Holy Spirit that guides us on this journey. With this assurance in mind, I can never let go of hope. Hope is what we believe, expect, and live, as seen in our actions and also in our words. I remain hopeful despite the challenges I may encounter on the journey. This is the hope that recharges us each day for the mission we are on and propels us on the way. Therefore, let us remain hopeful as we greet each new day.

May the God of hope fill you with all joy and peace in believing, so that by the power of the Holy Spirit you may abound in hope...

Romans 15:13

Dear God, thank you for Your abiding presence that dwells in me and fills me with hope; may my hope be a shining light to encourage others on this journey...Amen.

#27

Awaiting the Calm Within the Storm

There are times when events and situations seem to be out of my control, so I must step back and watch the hand of God at work. I withdraw emotionally, focusing on my breathing to relax as I remind myself of the serenity prayer attributed to St. Francis of Assisi. I kept this prayer on the wall facing me at my desk, which I often recited, asking God to give me the serenity to accept those things that I cannot change and to give me the courage to change the things that I can change, and most of all asking for wisdom to know the difference. Here I watch God at work and often it is through me; I am amazed sometimes at the outcome, but then I am quickly reminded that God works through us as His vessels. God is in the midst of all our storms of life and is ready to come to our aid and respond to all our needs. God will calm whatever storms we face. When we call out to God in faith, we can expect to see peace and calm within the confusion and chaos.

Be still and know that I am God. **Psalm 46:10**

Dear God, thank you for Your abiding peace to calm my spirit, even during times of chaos. Help me to always remember that You are with me and that You promise to never leave me. Amen.

#28

Preparing for the Day

I n preparing for each day, I set my spiritual GPS to direct me on my path for the day. I start by first giving thanks for the day and for becoming the person that God is molding me to be; because I am aware that God is not yet finished with me. I then seek God's guidance and direction for my day: and for God to open the eyes of my heart for all human beings, irrespective of their race, creed, or color, and to see them as children of God and to respect the dignity of all humanity. I ask for wisdom in making the right decisions for all my actions in the care and support of patients, family, colleagues, and myself. I also pray for patience and understanding to wait on the will of God, which is already at work in my endeavors. I give thanks, knowing that God sees our needs even before we ask, but we have been reminded to ask and we will receive.

I will instruct you and teach you the way you should go **Psalm 32:8**

Dear God, in You, do I put my trust to guide my day and to lead me in the way I should go. Thank you for being my Shepherd and guide. Amen.

#29

Maintaining Our Way to Health and Wholeness

As we put ourselves on the frontline to battle the sickness and illnesses of this time, let us recall and provide self-care, as well as practice within our lives the concept of health, healing, and wholeness. Let us entertain healing thoughts for ourselves, be more aware of the things that take over our minds, and replace them with thoughts of health. Let us think of healthy organs and cells in our bodies, and give thanks as we name them one by one. We cannot see our internal organs, but it is our constant hope that they are all healthy and functioning at their optimal level. We will, therefore, provide the healing care to ourselves that we would give to our families, friends, and patients. Let us now promise ourselves to respond to the subtle cues and cries of our ailing bodies. Let us also practice healing activities. Therefore, may we always make time for medical checkups and all preventive care diagnostic procedures. Throughout this most challenging period in healthcare, we will make a special effort to think, provide, and practice healing within ourselves to be always ready and able to perform at our optimal levels.

For God's temple is holy and that temple you are.
1 Corinthians 3:17

Dear God, thank you for the body You gave to me. Keep me ever mindful that everything You make is good. Thank you for the continued renewal of cells in my body, as Your healing continues to flow through me, restoring every cell and organ that only You can see. Thank you for the blessings of health, healing, and wholeness... Amen.

#30

Seeking Help

M y daily prayer is to be of service to all God's children and ending with, "Lord, what will You have me do?" My deep desire to help others is what channeled me into a nursing career. I am an ever-ready helper for others and forget that there are times when I too need to seek help from others. There are times when others offer, and I believe that I am okay and can manage. An old aunt, also a nurse, once reminded me not to deprive anyone of the satisfaction that I get from helping others. In caring for myself, I must recognize the importance of seeking help at home, at work, and in my community commitments. Help is available for all aspects of our lives: physical, emotional, and spiritual. Just as medical checkups support our physical well-being, sharing with colleagues in support groups, chats, and even one on one with our mental health colleagues can support our emotional well-being. I find it most helpful to have a spiritual counselor to call on, and also to have the support of a spiritual community, wherever your faith preference leads. These are invaluable resources for the total well-being of any caregiver.

Ask and it will be given you; seek and you shall find; knock and it will be opened to you.
Matthew 7:7

Dear God, help me to be aware of my needs and to seek help as needed... Amen.

Helen Bhagwandin

EdD, DMin (hon), MSN, RN-BC.

H elen Bhagwandin EdD, DMin (hon), MSN, RN-BC Retired Nursing Professor and an active Board Certified Faith Community Nurse. Presented at national and international conferences. Nursing experiences include: Medical-Surgical, Emergency, Charge Nurse for Dialysis Center, and Hospital Supervisor. Education: Nursing Diploma from John Radcliff, Oxford, England, other degrees from University of Miami, Barry University in Miami Fl, and Nova Southeastern University. Recipient of numerous Professional and Community awards. Serves on various Community Boards, numerous community service awards including the US President's Community Service award; listed in International WHO is WHO in Professional and Business Women; the WHO is WHO in American Teachers; and recipient of an honorary Doctor of Ministry from Trinity Theological Seminary.

A Pandemic War

All wars must cease
So that we will have peace.
But how long must we fight
To put all things aright?
Fighting a lingering war
Against an enemy we greatly abhor
Ignites every ounce of energy
To eliminate this invisible enemy.
Fight on, fight on, do not give in to vexation
For very soon we will use the weapon of vaccination.

A Pandemic Prayer

O God, our Creator, and Defender protect us from the illnesses and hazards of this pandemic that threatens to destroy Your creation. Remove from us any carelessness or negligence, so that we may follow the scientific protocols to better care for ourselves and care for the health of others: through Thy Dear name we pray. Amen.

A Prayer For Nurses and Healthcare Workers

Thank you, Lord, for the courage and strength You give to our nurses and healthcare workers, as they risk their health to care for the health of others, even when denied proper protection. We thank You for their hearts of compassion, caring, and service to Your people. Put Your hedge of protection about them and keep them safe for thy name's sake. Amen.

Reflections

_____

_____

_____

_____

_____

_____

_____

_____

_____

_____

_____

_____

_____

_____

CPSIA information can be obtained
at www.ICGtesting.com
Printed in the USA
BVHW052326260821
615309BV00018B/890